Grasshoppers
PHOTOS AND FACTS FOR EVERYONE

BY ISIS GAILLARD

Learn With Facts Series

Book 135

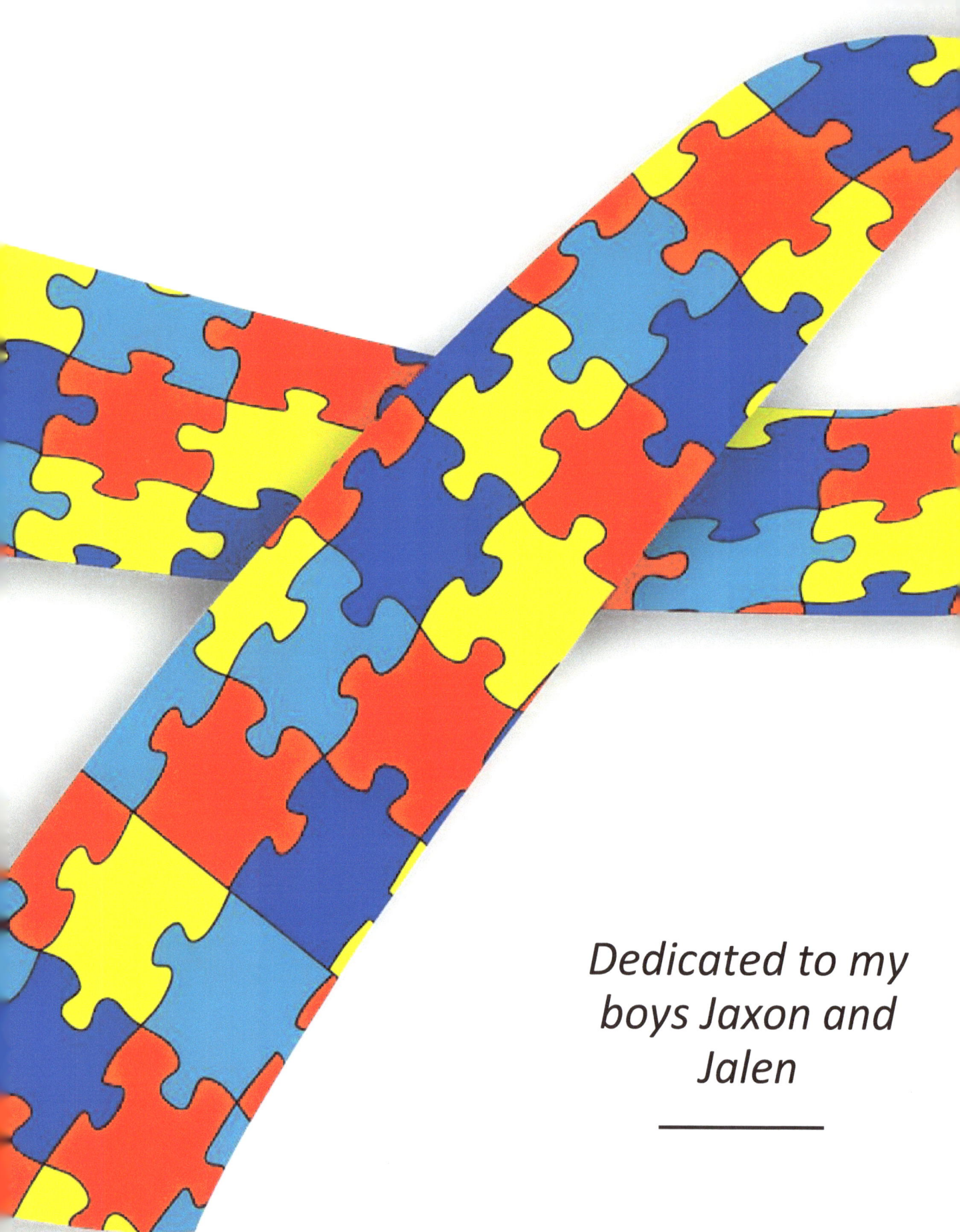

Dedicated to my boys Jaxon and Jalen

_____

CONTENTS

Image Credits: Royalty-free images reproduced under license from various stock image repositories.

Isis Gaillard. Grasshoppers: Photos and Facts for Everyone (Learn With Facts Series Book 135). Ebook Edition. Learn With Facts an imprint of TLM Media LLC

eISBN: 979-8-88700-834-9
ISBN-13: 979-8-88700-157-9

Introduction

Grasshopper, any of a group of jumping insects (suborder Caelifera) that are found in a variety of habitats. Grasshoppers occur in greatest numbers in lowland tropical forests, semiarid regions, and grasslands. They range in colour from green to olive or brown and may have yellow or red markings.

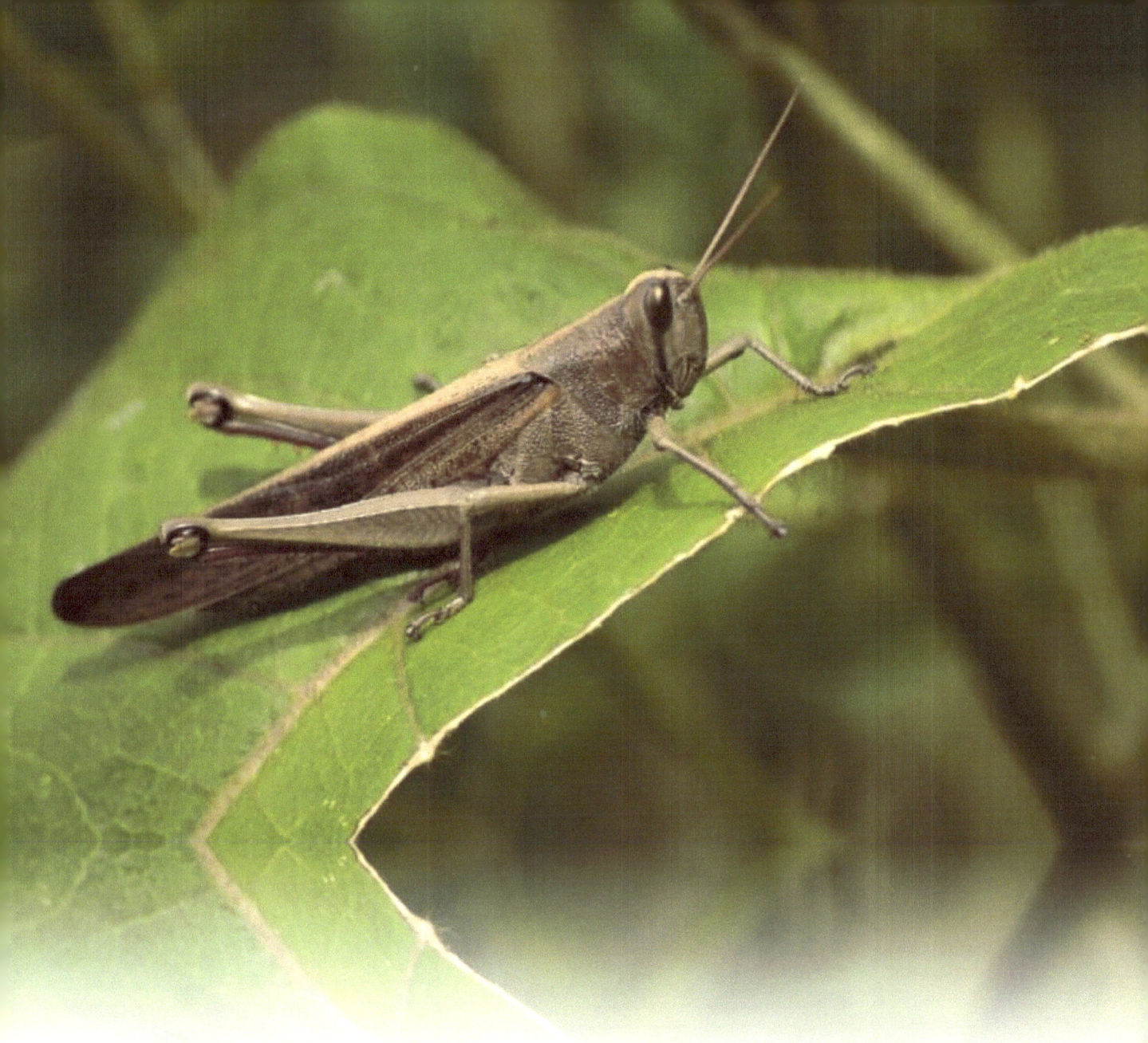

As hemimetabolous insects, they do not undergo complete metamorphosis; they hatch from an egg into a nymph or "hopper" which undergoes five moults, becoming more similar to the adult insect at each developmental stage.

Grasshoppers are beneficial and play a critical role in the environment by making it a more efficient place for plants and other animals to thrive. They facilitate a natural balance in the decomposing and regrowth process of plants.

They discovered that grasshoppers (Orthoptera: Acrididae) hail not from Africa, as commonly thought, but from South America, where they arose 59 million years ago. Over tens of millions of years, grasshoppers migrated, likely by flight, to colonize the continents.

A grasshopper lives up to a year if it is not hunted down by its predators. Within this time they complete their entire life cycle from birth to the embryo stage to nymph stage and finally as a full-grown adult. The majority of their life cycle is spent as nymphs, so an adult grasshopper only gets 30 days to live.

After pairing up, the smaller male grasshopper usually mounts the female and the female curls her abdomen up to reach the male's reproductive organ (aedeagus) from which she receives a package of sperm called a spermatophore. The mating process can take from 45 minutes to more than a day, depending on the species.

Description

Grasshoppers are medium to large insects. Adult length is 1 to 7 cm, depending on the species. Like their relatives the katydids and crickets, they have chewing mouthparts, two pairs of wings, one narrow and tough, the other wide and flexible, and long hind legs for jumping.

Grasshopper suddenly remembered that he saw its neighbour ants storing food for the winters

'The Ant and the Grasshopper' teaches us about putting work before play because it's more important to do the things you need to before doing the things you want to. In contrast to the last theme, maybe you know someone who's all work, work, work all the time.

Grasshoppers usually are a shade of brown, green or black. They have large hind legs that help them jump long distances, hence their name. Adult grasshoppers also have two sets of wings, with the forewings being slender and the hindwings large.

Grasshoppers are typically ground-dwelling insects with powerful hind legs which allow them to escape from threats by leaping vigorously.

Size

Indeed grasshoppers and crickets have pretty strong wings that allow them to travel long distances in search of food and or mates. Besides long distance travel, grasshoppers can also fly pretty high for their size and weight,

Grasshoppers are medium to large insects. Adult length is 1 to 7 cm, depending on the species. Like their relatives the katydids and crickets, they have chewing mouthparts, two pairs of wings, one narrow and tough, the other wide and flexible, and long hind legs for jumping.

Most grasshopper individuals grow to about 2 inches long although larger grasshoppers are found on a fairly regular basis that grow to more than 5 inches in length. The grasshopper has wings meaning it can migrate over long distances when the weather gets too cold.

Breeding

It is very easy to breed grasshoppers as long as you keep them in the right circumstances. They really need high temperature, low humidity and plenty of fresh food. If you have males and females, breeding will occur naturally. You don't need to move the eggs or nymphs to a different container.

Typically, a female grasshopper will lay about 100 eggs during the summer and fall. Outbreaks are favored when females produce more eggs as a result of better food quality and/or an extended period in the fall to lay eggs.

In the summer, the female grasshopper lays the fertilized egg pod, using her ovipositor and abdomen to insert the eggs about one to two inches underground, although they can also be laid in plant roots or even manure and usually in their habitats. These are immediately incubated.

Incomplete Metamorphosis Has Three Stages: Egg, Nymph, and Adult. In grasshopper metamorphosis, you can see that young grasshoppers (1-5) look very similar to the adults (6) as they grow larger.

The grasshopper life cycle only has three stages: egg, nymph, and adult. Grasshopper eggs are laid in the ground in pods that can contain a few to more than 100 eggs. In the spring, the nymphs come out of their eggs, eat, and molt, shedding their exoskeleton as they grow.

During grasshopper mating, the male grasshopper inserts his aedeagus into the female's ovipositor and deposits a spermatophore. When the female's eggs are fertilized, she will use her ovipositor to deposit them into the soil in egg pods.

Although grasshoppers complete only one generation a year, eggs hatch over a long period of time. Development from egg to adult requires about 40-60 days. Also, eggs of different species hatch at different times so small grashoppers can be found throughout the growing season.

Eating Habit

Birds are one of the most important natural predators of grasshoppers. These insects feature in the diets of dozens of bird species including blue jays, owls, crows, blackbirds, sparrows, wrens, robins, bluebirds, meadowlarks, and more.

Grasshoppers Provide Disease-Fighting Antioxidants To make them edible, the wings and legs are removed. They are high in protein and fat, but low in carbohydrates, according to the aforementioned Food Science of Animal Resources review. In Japan, people eat them fried with soy sauce.

Eating Habit

Grasshoppers primarily eat grasses, leaves, and other plants. If plants are scarce, some species will start eating moss, rotting meat, and other insects, but they greatly prefer leafy greens and vegetables. If you have a garden or farm, grasshoppers can be serious pests that eat your entire crop.

Interesting Facts

1. Grasshoppers and locusts are the same thing.
2. Grasshoppers have ears on their bellies. In grasshoppers, the auditory organs are in a rather unusual location – on the abdomen.
3. Although grasshoppers can hear, they can't distinguish pitches very well.
4. Grasshoppers make music by stridulating or crepitating. That sounds complicated, doesn't it?
5. Grasshoppers can fly. Because grasshoppers have such powerful jumping legs, people sometimes don't realize they have wings, too!
6. Grasshoppers jump by catapulting themselves into the air. If you've ever tried to catch a grasshopper, you know how far they can jump to flee danger.
7. Grasshoppers cause billions of dollars in damage to food crops annually, worldwide.
8. Grasshoppers provide an important source of protein to people in many parts of the world.

THE END

Thanks for reading facts about Grasshoppers. I am a parent of two boys on the autism spectrum. I am always advocating for Autism Spectrum Disorders which part of the proceeds of this book goes to many Non-Profit Autism Organizations. I would love if you would leave a review.

Author Note from Isis Gaillard:

Thanks For Reading! I hope you enjoyed the fact book about Grasshoppers.

Please check out all the Learn With Facts and the Kids Learn With Pictures series available.

Visit www.IsisGaillard.com and www.LearnWithFacts.com to find more books in the Learn With Facts Series

More Books In The Series

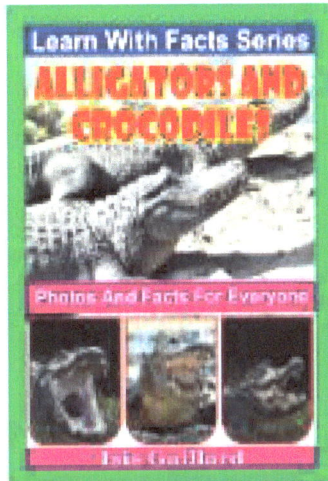

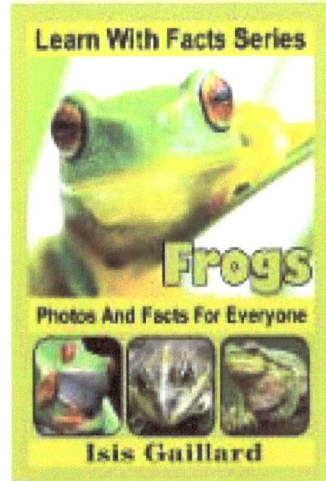

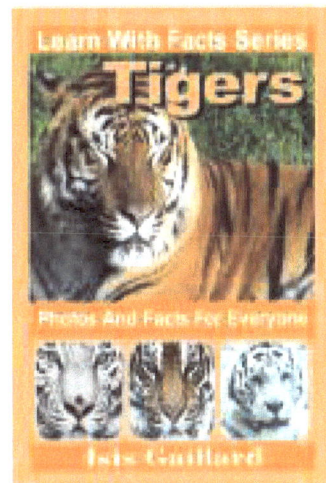

Over 75 books in the Learn With Facts Series.

Set 1

```
A  L  L  X  R  F  K  Y  S  A  S  I  X  K  P
S  Q  H  Y  N  O  W  O  G  R  B  G  S  O  W
E  L  X  D  B  X  O  B  A  I  A  D  O  R  R
L  G  W  B  Z  E  U  Y  T  L  R  G  F  R  D
E  K  G  O  O  S  B  X  Z  I  A  V  U  U  F
P  L  D  W  H  I  E  H  B  E  I  S  Y  O  S
H  S  D  V  I  C  E  C  T  E  Y  W  C  H  C
A  C  H  I  N  C  H  I  L  L  A  S  A  I  J
N  S  S  B  N  N  F  A  F  J  L  T  Y  A  L
T  O  E  U  T  O  F  P  M  V  E  D  C  I  S
S  O  D  S  M  F  S  V  T  E  R  S  O  W  R
E  R  Z  O  R  A  G  A  H  Y  L  N  Q  V  A
A  A  F  E  L  O  T  C  U  I  S  E  Q  Y  E
G  G  Q  R  G  P  H  O  K  R  A  K  O  L  B
L  N  T  C  X  X  H  Z  P  F  S  E  A  N  B
E  A  L  I  S  E  L  I  D  O  C  O  R  C  S
S  K  D  E  K  V  W  S  N  D  P  N  D  Z  I
S  G  O  H  E  G  D  E  H  S  O  P  F  G  I
F  H  S  R  E  V  A  E  B  P  C  C  I  B  S
A  H  B  P  E  G  I  R  A  F  F  E  S  H  E
```

Word List

Bears	Dolphins	Kangaroos
Beavers	Eagles	Koalas
Birds	Elephants	Lions
Chameleons	Foxes	Owls
Cheetahs	Frogs	
Chinchillas	Giraffes	
Cougars	Hedgehogs	
Crocodiles	Hippopotamus	
Dinosaurs	Horses	

Set 2

```
Z  G  K  M  V  B  E  E  S  S  O  V  E  E  P
P  E  A  C  O  C  K  S  F  R  A  N  E  Y  H
G  I  P  Z  A  L  L  I  G  A  T  O  R  S  B
C  J  G  A  E  N  F  V  S  U  U  L  Y  C  R
Y  R  R  U  N  L  X  Z  R  G  Q  K  C  S  C
H  S  I  F  A  D  L  Y  E  A  N  O  E  I  K
R  P  C  D  H  N  A  E  G  J  T  I  P  H  S
H  I  F  A  N  W  A  S  I  X  P  O  X  N  S
I  D  Z  A  M  A  P  S  T  P  Q  I  E  A  Y
N  E  F  L  H  E  S  B  U  X  T  T  R  G  H
O  R  L  P  G  M  L  P  T  O  T  B  B  S  S
C  S  A  A  U  M  D  S  A  I  E  A  L  E  I
E  A  M  C  E  N  W  S  K  Z  T  C  R  A  F
R  A  I  A  A  U  N  D  M  S  R  T  W  T  Y
O  L  N  S  S  I  N  K  S  E  F  F  V  U  L
S  J  G  Z  U  A  V  E  N  R  R  T  K  R  L
G  O  O  G  S  O  C  B  A  H  S  I  A  T  E
D  I  N  T  F  C  B  Y  K  Q  Z  C  B  L  J
B  E  A  Q  B  U  T  T  E  R  F  L  I  E  S
P  C  I  N  S  E  C  T  S  E  V  Q  K  S  Z
```

Word List

Alligators	Flamingo	Penguins
Alpacas	Gazelle	Rhinoceros
Bats	Hyena	Sea Turtles
Bees	Iguanas	Snakes
Butterflies	Insects	Spiders
Camels	Jaguars	Tigers
Cats and Kittens	Jellyfish	Zebras
Dogs and Puppies	Pandas	
Fish	Peacocks	

Set 3

```
P  S  G  U  K  P  O  N  I  E  S  C  M  M  S
O  A  N  S  O  C  T  O  P  U  S  E  S  I  E
T  T  R  O  E  R  O  O  S  T  E  R  S  Q  A
C  S  K  R  I  F  K  K  J  M  Y  P  W  S  L
M  Y  J  A  O  P  O  V  J  L  C  I  A  G  S
W  K  C  Q  E  T  R  W  E  S  U  G  N  G  A
H  Z  E  F  I  Y  S  O  R  A  V  S  S  O  N
W  O  L  V  E  S  P  A  C  E  S  A  S  S  D
L  G  Y  Z  W  A  E  S  S  S  Y  N  W  T  S
V  X  T  L  R  B  D  O  N  D  O  D  N  R  E
H  G  I  D  R  R  O  A  Y  G  S  P  S  I  A
W  E  S  A  A  M  C  G  A  T  T  I  E  C  L
U  H  L  Z  X  I  G  R  P  A  A  G  A  H  I
L  O  I  E  L  T  D  E  K  B  R  L  H  E  O
P  L  O  E  X  O  U  R  I  S  F  E  O  S  N
L  N  P  Q  D  A  E  R  D  G  I  T  R  N  S
B  R  P  O  V  E  S  W  T  X  S  S  S  V  S
A  E  M  L  M  L  Y  N  X  L  H  T  E  W  G
D  O  O  X  X  O  W  H  A  L  E  S  S  H  M
K  V  R  A  N  T  E  A  T  E  R  S  A  J  T
```

Word List

Anteater	Parrots	Starfish
Komodo Dragons	Pelicans	Swans
Leopards	Pigs and Piglets	Turtles
Lizards	Polar Bears	Whales
Lynx	Ponies	Wolves
Meerkat	Roosters	
Moose	Scorpions	
Octopuses	Seahorses	
Ostriches	Seals and Sea Lions	

Set 4

```
Z  P  O  R  C  U  P  I  N  E  S  C  M  F  Z
P  K  N  S  K  C  E  O  Y  U  H  A  O  A  I
E  C  H  I  D  N  A  R  F  M  O  E  U  A  H
K  H  C  K  W  Q  E  E  S  E  R  R  N  K  F
R  M  P  L  S  E  U  K  Y  G  O  A  T  S  X
N  A  R  L  D  Q  R  J  N  E  C  H  A  P  V
S  H  C  N  A  O  U  U  G  B  H  P  I  B  L
T  Y  I  C  T  T  P  I  U  B  I  L  N  B  I
C  E  E  S  O  F  Y  F  R  E  C  T  L  Z  V
R  O  G  K  E  O  F  P  Z  R  K  D  I  S  E
F  D  W  I  N  A  N  L  U  R  E  O  O  L  D
E  W  I  S  L  O  G  S  L  S  N  L  N  O  N
R  E  T  O  V  V  D  X  U  A  S  G  S  T  A
R  C  H  I  P  M  U  N  K  S  M  W  W  H  I
E  W  S  H  A  R  K  S  D  Q  S  A  M  S  N
T  I  D  Y  C  Z  O  O  T  H  O  R  A  D  A
S  Y  T  E  G  U  I  N  E  A  P  I  G  S  M
J  S  E  T  E  S  E  E  R  D  L  O  J  T  S
J  K  H  H  F  R  P  S  K  U  N  K  S  N  A
X  A  R  M  A  D  I  L  L  O  C  E  R  L  T
```

Word List

Armadillo
Buffalo
Chickens
Chipmunks
Cows
Deer
Donkeys
Echidna
Emu

Ferrets
Goats
Guinea Pigs
Llama
Mountain Lions
Platypus
Porcupines
Raccoons
Reindeer

Sharks
Sheep
Skunks
Sloths
Squirrels
Storks
Tasmanian Devil

Set 5

```
3  W  M  S  E  S  I  O  T  R  O  T  T  X  M
0  Q  M  A  R  S  U  P  I  A  L  S  S  S  V
D  B  G  Z  R  J  A  D  D  G  V  B  C  E  A
A  A  V  V  H  I  S  L  A  M  M  A  M  T  N
N  S  L  A  M  I  N  A  M  R  A  F  S  O  T
G  B  J  B  K  X  S  E  Y  O  X  R  M  Y  E
E  G  A  E  T  U  X  K  L  P  X  I  U  O  L
R  P  U  M  R  N  C  F  S  I  C  C  S  C  O
O  C  U  L  O  A  O  L  R  B  F  T  S  F  P
U  M  A  F  T  J  E  U  S  V  R  E  O  Y  E
S  W  V  T  F  S  I  R  B  A  E  I  P  A  S
A  C  L  M  A  I  U  U  M  D  P  J  O  A  A
N  E  X  E  I  M  N  P  A  N  T  H  E  R  S
I  M  W  G  E  M  H  S  I  T  I  H  B  D  G
M  X  T  L  P  I  Y  F  B  U  L  T  N  V  R
A  J  A  D  B  G  A  S  Q  R  E  B  C  A  L
L  T  D  I  Y  B  K  N  R  K  S  Q  W  R  B
S  P  A  P  V  O  S  O  J  E  S  W  F  K  D
U  N  V  B  N  O  D  L  G  Y  S  J  V  S  Y
S  J  G  O  R  I  L  L  A  S  A  S  A  E  H
```

Word List

30 Dangerous Animals
Aardvarks
Amphibians
Antelopes
Cattle
Coyotes
Farm Animals
Gorillas
Lemurs

Mammals
Marine Life
Marsupials
Opossums
Panthers
Puffins
Reptiles
Tortoises
Turkeys

Walrus
Weasels
Yaks

Set 1

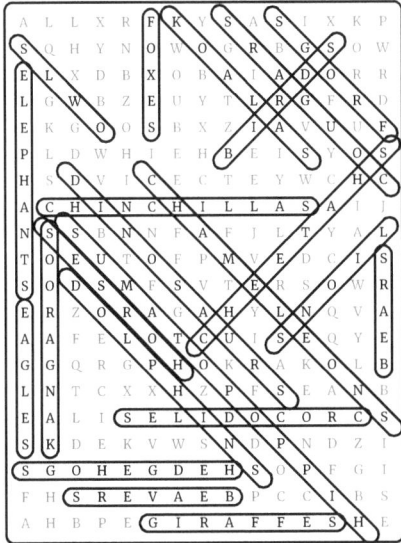

Set 2

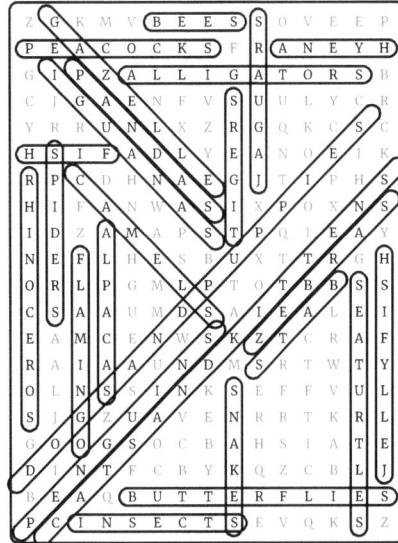

Set 3

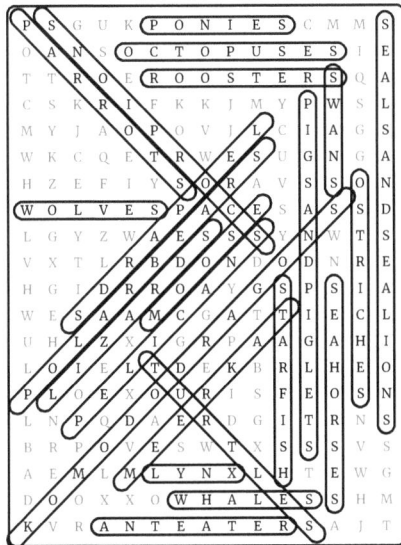

Set 4

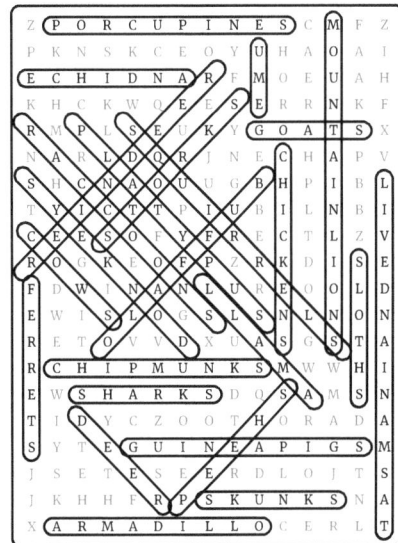

Set 5

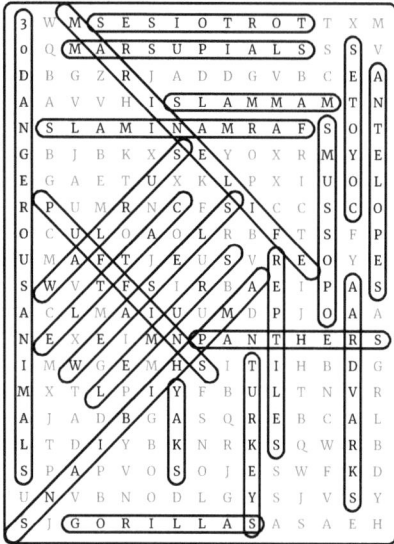

Puzzle 1

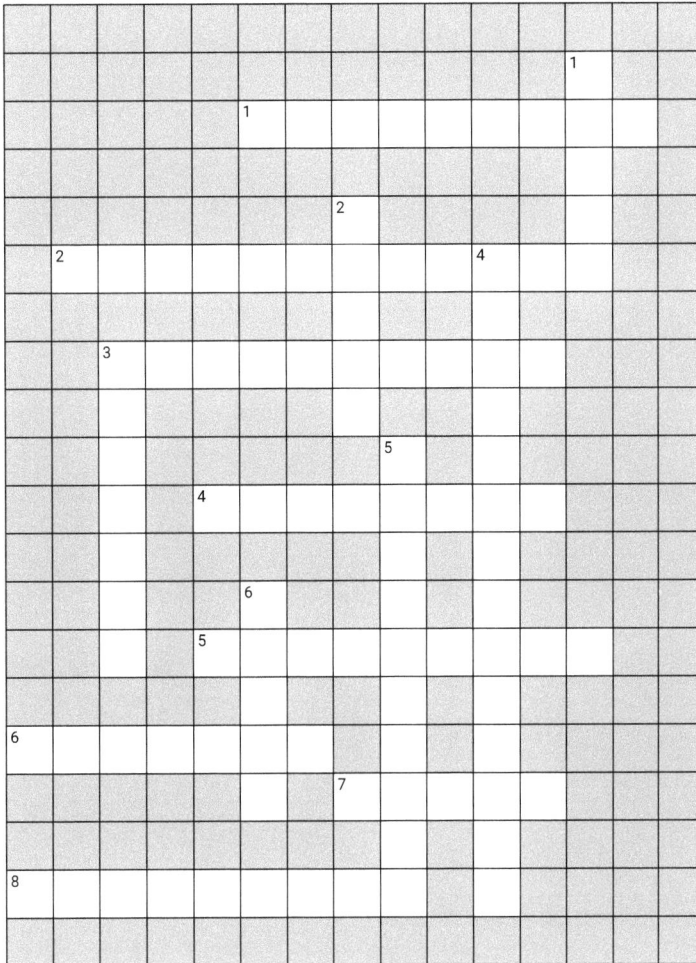

ACROSS
1. Dinosaurs
2. Caterpillars
3. Crocodiles
4. Dolphins
5. Hedgehogs
6. Beavers
7. Foxes
8. Elephants

DOWN
1. Frogs
2. Birds
3. Cougars
4. Apes and Monkeys
5. Chameleons
6. Bears

Puzzle 2

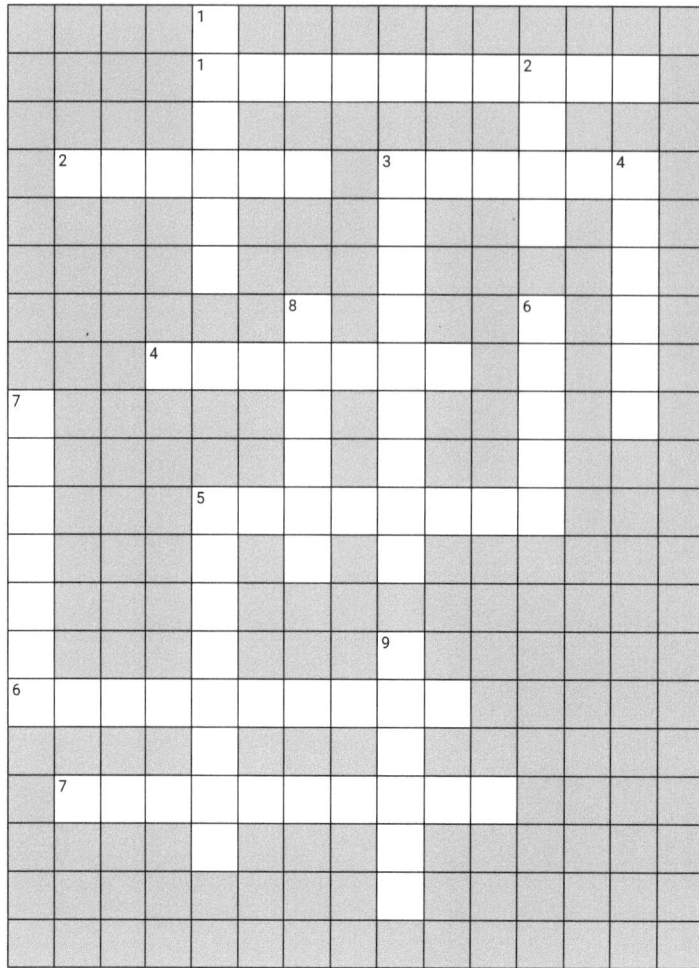

ACROSS
1. Alligators
2. Tigers
3. Koalas
4. Alpacas
5. Peacocks
6. Sea Turtles
7. Rhinoceros

DOWN
1. Camels
2. Owls
3. Kangaroos
4. Snakes
5. Penguins
6. Lions
7. Spiders
8. Pandas
9. Zebras

Puzzle 3

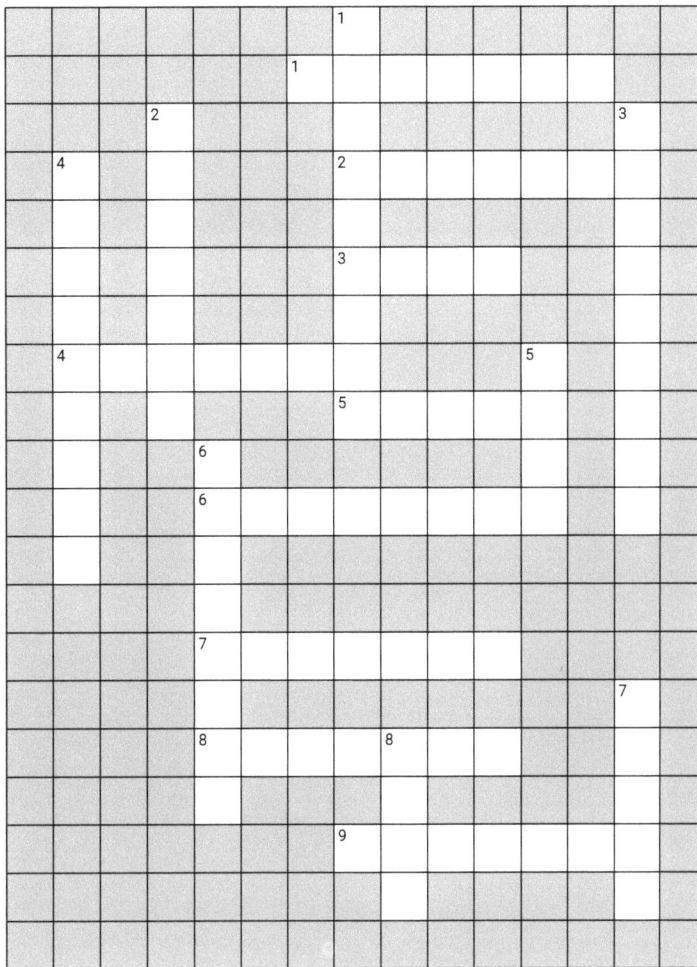

ACROSS
1. Meerkat
2. Lizards
3. Fish
4. Parrots
5. Hyena
6. Leopards
7. Iguanas
8. Gazelle
9. Insects

DOWN
1. Jellyfish
2. Jaguars
3. Ostriches
4. Octopuses
5. Bats
6. Flamingo
7. Moose
8. Lynx

Puzzle 4

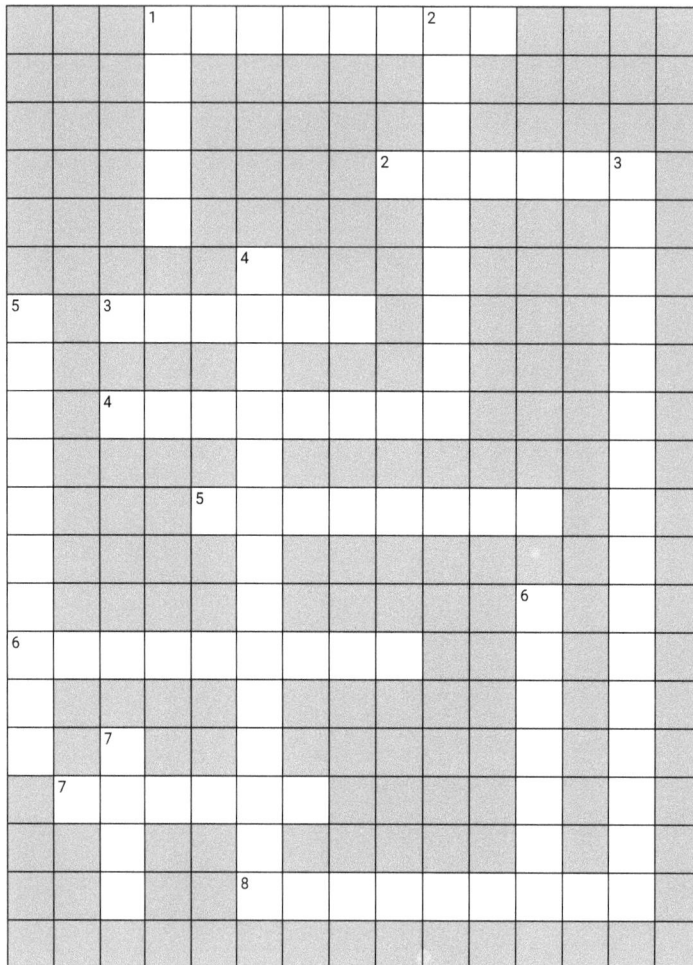

ACROSS
1. Starfish
2. Whales
3. Ponies
4. Roosters
5. Anteater
6. Armadillo
7. Wolves
8. Scorpions

DOWN
1. Swans
2. Seahorses
3. Seals and Sea Lions
4. Pigs and Piglets
5. Polar Bears
6. Buffalo
7. Cows

Puzzle 5

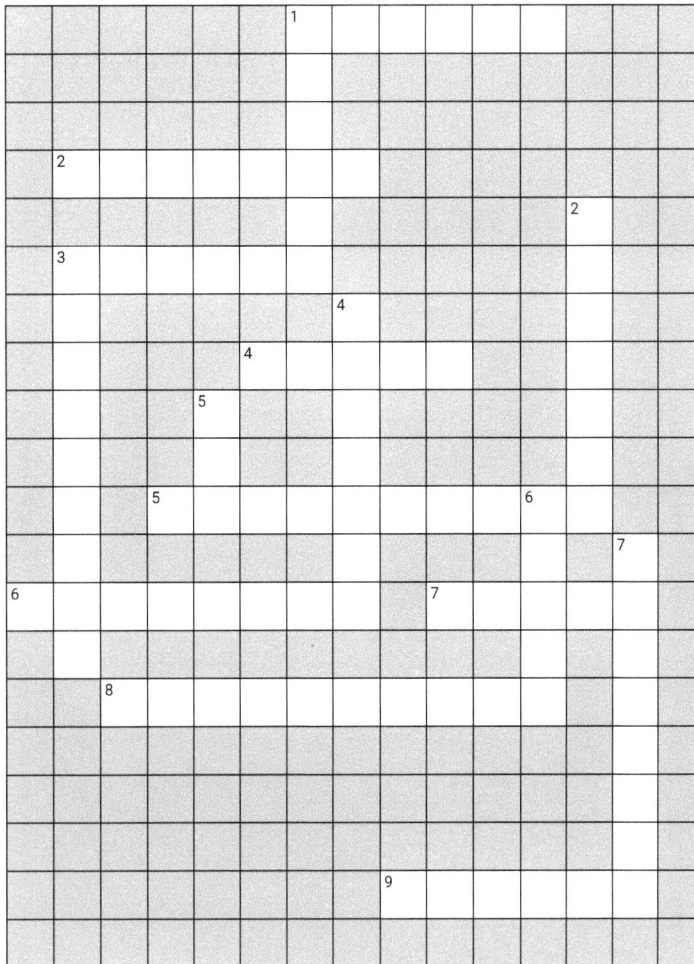

ACROSS
1. Sloths
2. Echidna
3. Storks
4. Sheep
5. Guinea Pigs
6. Platypus
7. Llama
8. Porcupines
9. Sharks

DOWN
1. Skunks
2. Donkeys
3. Squirrels
4. Ferrets
5. Emu
6. Goats
7. Raccoons

Puzzle 6

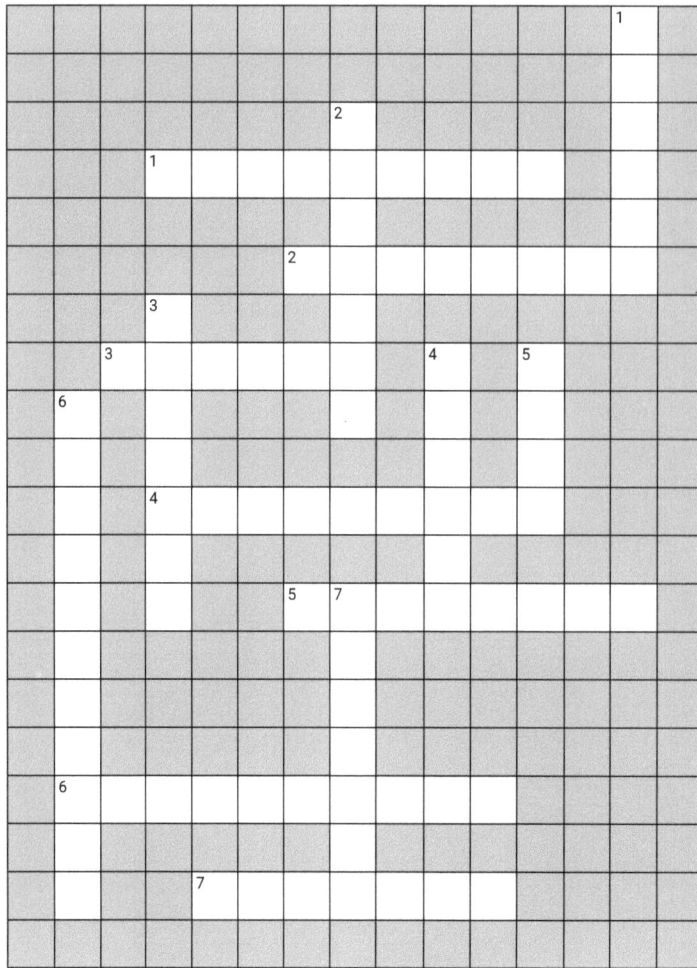

ACROSS
1. Tortoises
2. Gorillas
3. Cattle
4. Aardvarks
5. Opossums
6. Amphibians
7. Weasels

DOWN
1. Lemurs
2. Coyotes
3. Mammals
4. Walrus
5. Yaks
6. Farm Animals
7. Puffins

Puzzle 1

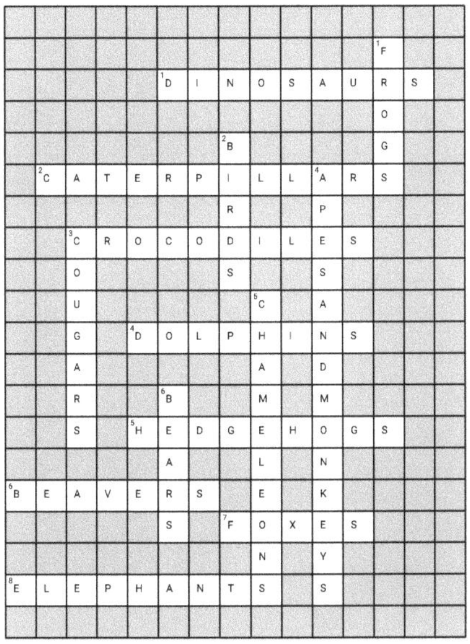

1 FROGS
1 DINOSAURS
2 BIRDS
2 CATERPILLARS
3 CROCODILES
3 COUGARS
4 APES AND MONKEYS
4 DOLPHINS
5 CHAMELEONS
5 HEDGEHOGS
6 BEARS
6 BEAVERS
7 FOXES
8 ELEPHANTS

Puzzle 2

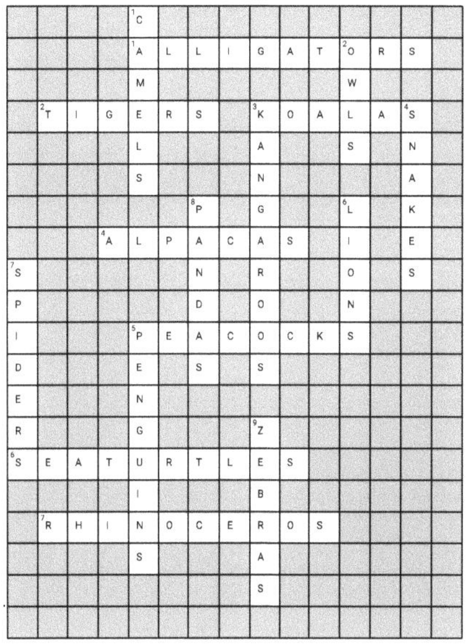

1 CAMELS
1 ALLIGATORS
2 OWLS
2 TIGERS
3 KANGAROOS
3 KOALAS
4 SNAKES
4 ALPACAS
5 PENGUINS
5 PEACOCKS
6 LIONS
6 SEA TURTLES
7 SPIDERS
7 RHINOCEROS
8 PANDAS
9 ZEBRAS

Puzzle 3

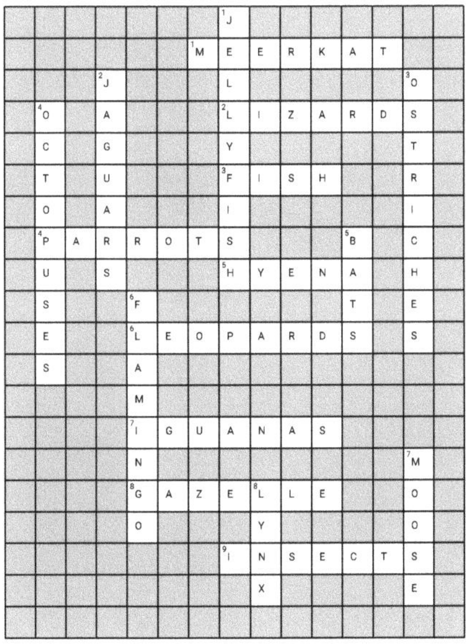

1 JELLYFISH
1 MEERKAT
2 JAGUARS
2 LIZARDS
3 OSTRICHES
3 FISH
4 OCTOPUSES
4 PARROTS
5 BATS
5 HYENA
6 FLAMINGO
6 LEOPARDS
7 IGUANAS
7 MOOSE
8 GAZELLE
8 LYNX
9 INSECTS

Puzzle 4

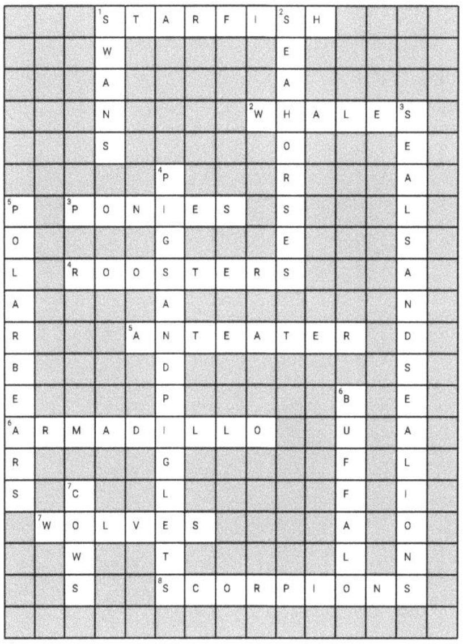

1 STARFISH
1 SWANS
2 SEAHORSES
2 WHALES
3 SEALS AND SEA LIONS
3 PONIES
4 PIGS AND PIGLETS
4 ROOSTERS
5 POLAR BEARS
5 ANTEATER
6 BUFFALO
6 ARMADILLO
7 COWS
7 WOLVES
8 SCORPIONS

Puzzle 5

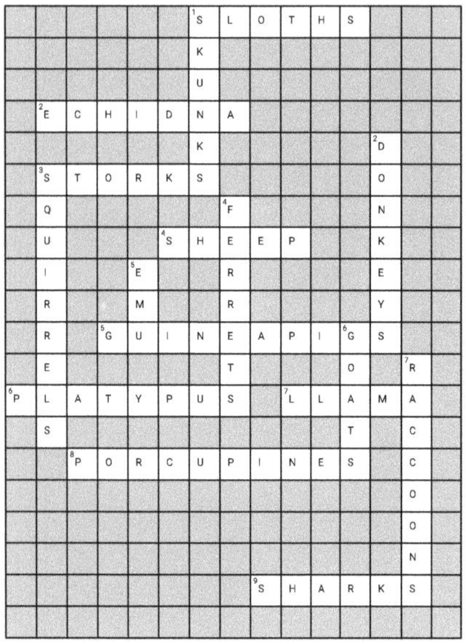

Across and down answers in crossword grid:

- SLOTHS
- SKUNK
- ECHIDNA
- DONKEY
- STORKS
- SQUIRREL
- SHEEP
- FERRETS
- EMU
- GUINEAPIGS
- GOOSE
- PLATYPUS
- LLAMA
- RACCOON
- PORCUPINES
- SHARKS

Puzzle 6

Across and down answers in crossword grid:

- LEMUR
- TORTOISES
- COYOTE
- GORILLAS
- MMM
- CATTLE
- WALRUS
- YAK
- FAMILIARS
- AARDVARKS
- OPOSSUMS
- STUFFUN
- AMPHIBIANS
- WEASELS

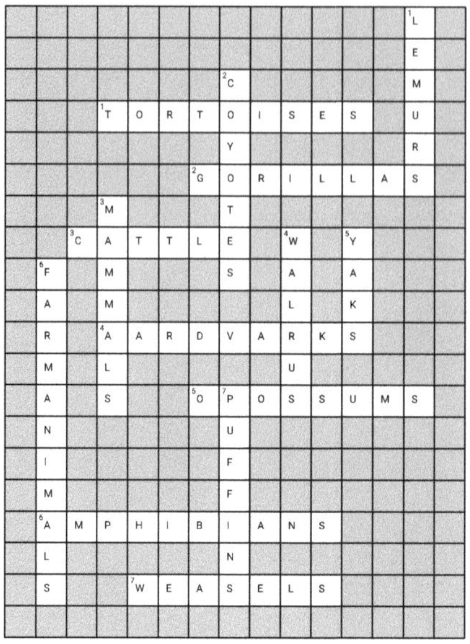

www.ingramcontent.com/pod-product-compliance
Lightning Source LLC
Chambersburg PA
CBHW060825270326
41931CB00002B/71